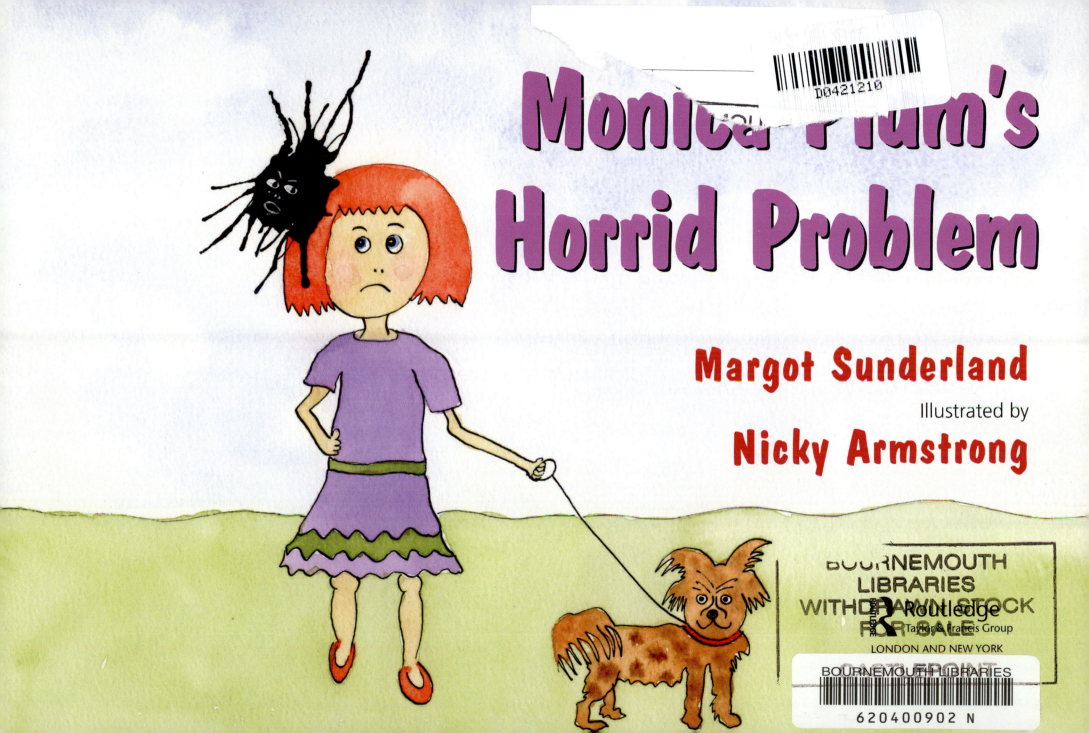

Monica Plum's Horrid Problem

Margot Sunderland

Illustrated by

Nicky Armstrong

Routledge
Taylor & Francis Group

LONDON AND NEW YORK

Monica Plum had a Horrid Problem.

Wherever Monica went, it came too.

It got under her pillow, so she couldn't sleep properly.

It got into her dreams, so they turned into nightmares.

It got into her school time, so she couldn't learn.

It even got into her homework, so she made lots of mistakes.

People tried to help Monica.

The help didn't help.

Some people said," *Smile Monica.*

Everything will be better if you just forget your worries."

They didn't understand Monica Plum's Horrid Problem.

Sometimes Monica felt like a tiny dot.

Sometimes she felt like a monster because she got so angry.

Sometimes she shook with fear.

"*It's no fun being me,*" thought Monica.

One day at school, Mrs. Peters asked everyone to draw a home.

Most of the children drew warmly lit rooms and happy faced people.

Monica drew a house of smashed-up things.

One room was full of fighting; the next, full of fear;

Another, full of tears like rain, so the roof fell in.

But Monica's drawing was not the only different one.

Billy drew a house covered in fog.

Fin drew one with a crocodile in the bathroom.

And Chloe's house had a great big crack, right down the middle.

Billy

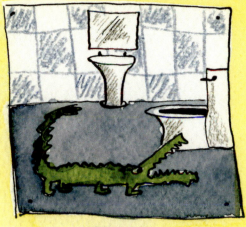

Fin

Monica

Chloe

At playtime Monica went to find Billy, Fin and Chloe.

"I saw your drawings," she said. *"I wonder if you have Horrid Problems that get into your homework and your dreams."*

Billy and Fin nodded, but Chloe said,

" 'Course not stupid," and ran off to find her friends.

That night, Monica had a dream about children trying to carry grown-ups.

It was hard, but somehow they managed.

Other children carried huge bags and suitcases.

It was hard, but somehow they managed.

One day, Mrs. Peters took Monica to one side.

"Monica, I can see you're not happy. Will you tell me about it?"

Monica shook her head. How could she possibly do that?

That might make the Horrid Problem even more horrid!

But Monica was pleased that Mrs. Peters didn't just say *"Cheer up!"* like everyone else.

Mrs. Peters went on, *"Monica, you need a Knight."*

Monica didn't really know what a Knight was!

"Knights are fearless in fighting for fairness", explained Mrs Peters.

"Knights take you by the hand and don't let go.

Knights will be with you all the way,

until you feel safe and warm inside.

And some knights are disguised as ordinary people."

Monica was feeling so safe with Mrs. Peters

that she spoke about her dream.

Mrs. Peters listened carefully then said,

"I think your dream might be about children carrying problems

that belong to grown-ups. I will help you find a Knight.

Go to that old bike shed in the playground.

Someone's written 'WHISPER' in one of the corners.

Trace your hand over the letters."

Monica rushed to tell Billy and Fin about the Knights
and the WHISPER in the bike shed.
They waited until lunchtime.
Fin spotted the WHISPER under a huge cobweb.
They traced their fingers over the letters.

Hey presto! The back of the bike shed
opened onto a brand new world.
There were fairy lights and bright candles,
and a great big sign saying, *"Whispering Wood, this way"*.
They followed it; they weren't frightened.
The air felt warm and good.

Along the way there were lots of children
carrying heavy baggage, just like in Monica's dream.
"I wonder why they're here?" thought Monica.
The trees heard her, *"Because, like you Monica,*
they're carrying big problems," whispered one.
"But the wood will help, it's full of Knights."

Sure enough, when Monica looked around
there were knights everywhere and some ordinary-looking grown-ups too.
Monica remembered what Mrs. Peters had said:
Knights disguised as ordinary people.

"Welcome," said Red Knight. "We're here to help you with your problems.

You've been carrying them around for far too long.

They fly around your minds like bats, spoiling your happiness.

Best way to let the bats out is by talking to someone about them.

Then they'll stop bothering you so much."

Like magic, a long washing line of drawings appeared.

Monica saw *her* drawing right in the middle.

There they were again, all those smashed-up things:

the fighting, the fear, the tears like rain.

One by one the children talked about their drawings:

"In mine, volcanoes are going off all the time."

"In mine, there are horrible sleeping things. We mustn't wake them."

"In mine, everyone's only all right if they have some alcohol to drink."

"Mine is full of far away people with far away faces."

"When my house wobbles, the whole world wobbles."

Then it was Monica's turn:

"In mine, I sometimes feel like I'm losing me."

Children were nodding their heads.

For the first time, Monica felt she was not alone.

It felt so good to say what she'd never said before.

Overhead, she saw some bats flying off, way into the distance.

"I try so hard to mend the broken people," said Fin.

"It's not your job to make things better," said Green Knight " That's for grown-ups to do."

Then a tough looking boy called Smithie piped up,

"Sometimes I do to little kids what's been done to me. I'm born bad."

"Not true," said Green Knight

"It's just that a nightmare got stuck in your brain,"

"Am I mad?" gulped a skinny kid called Sam.

"No," said Green Knight,

"If we're too alone from no one helping, it's maddening."

"But children, what about your cry of 'STOP'"? asked Red Knight.

"We have no voice," some of them replied. "We see what we don't want to see. We hear what we don't want to hear. But we can't say what we want to say."

"Not anymore," said Red Knight.

"We will help you find your voice. We will help you find your NO!"

With that, the Knights led the children to the top of Highest Hill.

They showed them how to shout their shock.

Billy screamed, *"I hate it when you fight."*

Then Fin, *"My heart breaks when I see you hurting"*

The children started to chant:

"*Stop the Hurting, Stop the Hurting, Stop the Hurting.*"

They roared their shock and pain, like strong lions.

How free they felt,

when in the past, they'd sometimes been afraid to breathe.

Then everything was calm and still.

For the first time ever, Monica felt as if she'd put down the baggage she'd been carrying for so very long.

Then Knight of Rolling River spoke:

"Now we must practise dealing with what life throws at you"

He led the children to the river and taught them to canoe.

Sometimes the canoes rolled over and they all fell out.

But that was funny, not scary, because they were together.

And because the Knights were always there to help.

Storms came.

Knights showed them how to build shelters.

Thunder clapped.

Knights showed them how to shout back.

Floods came.

Knights showed them how to build a raft.

It was hard, but Monica loved every minute because they were doing it TOGETHER.

Then back through Whispering Wood, to a lovely campfire.

Oldest Knight spoke, and all fell silent.

"Living with Horrid Problems is like battling storms and floods and thunder.

But you've seen how different it can feel when you have a friend."

"I get it!" shouted Monica,

"Together means the sun will shine for you again."

"Excellent Monica!" said Red Knight.

"We have two more important things to show you," said Oldest Knight.

When the children looked up, they saw a terrible thing.

All their drawings in one huge Horrid House:

The big crack, the volcanoes, the glaring eyes,

the wobbling that makes the world wobble,

the sleeping horrible things, the far-away people with far-away faces.

Monica shivered and held Green Knight's hand.

"Now turn around," said Oldest Knight.

The children turned round and saw a meadow

with tall grass and a warm gentle breeze.

"Always remember. When you face your Great Big Problems,

you've got your back to the lovely things in the world.

So never forget to turn around."

The children practised looking at the Horrid House,
turning around, looking back, turning around again.
And then walking away,
into that meadow with the tall grass and the warm breeze.

They found slides and swings, paddling pools and sand castles.
They played like never before.

It was time to say goodbye.

"*Remember,*" said Red Knight.

"*There are always Knights around - if you wait and look.*

And one day, some of you will be Knights too."

The children were sad to leave.

But they were leaving richer and wiser, with new friends.

Several weeks later at school,

Monica watched a little boy she'd seen in Whispering Wood

going up to the Head Teacher and saying, *"I need a Knight.*

The help I'm getting is too small for my Big Problem."

The Head Teacher was lost for words.

"Excuse me sir," said Monica,

"Small-size help is fine for scraped knees and losing your favourite toy.

But it's not enough for great big problems that get into your sleep

and your schoolwork and spoil your life."

The Head Teacher shook his head, *"But there are no Knights here,"* he said.

"Then we will go and find one ourselves," said Monica.

And off they went, to do just that.